EDGAR ALLEN POE'S

The Tell-Tale Heart

Peter Leigh

Published in association with The Basic Skills Agency

Hodder & Stoughton

A MEMBER OF THE HODDER HEADLINE GROUP

Acknowledgements
Cover: Fred Van Deelan
Illustrations: Jim Eldridge
Photograph of Edgar Allen Poe © The Hulton Getty Picture Collection Limited

Orders: please contact Bookpoint Ltd, 39 Milton Park, Abingdon, Oxon OX14 4TD. Telephone: (44) 01235 400414, Fax: (44) 01235 400454. Lines are open from 9.00–6.00, Monday to Saturday, with a 24 hour message answering service. Email address: orders@bookpoint.co.uk

British Library Cataloguing in Publication Data
A catalogue record for this title is available from The British Library

ISBN 0 340 74313 1

First published 1999
Impression number 10 9 8 7 6 5 4 3 2 1
Year 2005 2004 2003 2002 2001 2000 1999

Typeset by Fakenham Photosetting Ltd, Fakenham, Norfolk.
Printed in Great Britain for Hodder & Stoughton Educational, a division of Hodder Headline Plc, 338 Euston Road, London NW1 3BH by Redwood Books, Trowbridge, Wiltshire.

About the author

Edgar Allan Poe was born in 1809,
and died in 1849.

He was a strange man,
haunted by strange dreams.

He wrote some famous horror stories,
and this is one of them.

About the story

The story is told by a man
who is deeply disturbed.

He tells us his own tale,
but we never know his name.

Nor do we know the name of the old man,
who is his victim.

I'm not mad.
Nervous, yes!
Very, very nervous.
But not mad.

My nerves have sharpened my senses,
not dulled them.
Especially my hearing.
I hear all things in heaven and earth.
I hear some things in hell.
So how can you call me mad?

Listen, I will tell you the whole story,
and you will hear how well I am,
how calm I am.

It is impossible to say
how the idea first entered my brain,
but once it was there,
it haunted me day and night.

Purpose? There was none!
Hatred? There was none!

I loved the old man.
He had never wronged me.
He had never insulted me.
I had no desire for his gold.

I think it was his eye.
Yes! That was it.

One of his eyes
looked like the eye of a vulture –
a pale blue eye,
with a film over it.

Whenever it looked at me,
my blood ran cold.
And so gradually, I made up my mind
to take the life of the old man,
and get rid of the eye for ever.

Now this is the point.
You think I'm mad.

But madmen know nothing,
and you should have seen *me*.
You should have seen how clever I was,
how carefully I prepared.

I was never kinder to the old man
than during the whole week
before I killed him.

Every night, about midnight,
I turned the latch of his door,
and opened it – oh, so gently!

And then,
when I had opened it
just wide enough for my head,
I pushed in a dark lantern,
all closed – closed
so that no light shone out.

Lanterns were lights that you could carry around, but they had shutters on them so you could close them right up.

And then I pushed in my head.

Oh, you would have laughed
to see how cleverly I pushed it in!

I moved it slowly – very, very slowly
– so that I would not disturb
the old man's sleep.
It took me an hour
to push my whole head
through the opening
so that I could see him
as he lay upon his bed.

Ha!
– would a madman
have been so clever as this?

And then,
when my head was well in the room,
I opened the lantern carefully –
oh, so carefully
– carefully because the hinges creaked.
I opened it just so much
that a single thin ray
fell upon the vulture eye.

the hinges of the shutter

And I did this for seven long nights,
every night just at midnight.
But I found the eye always closed.

And so I could not do the work,
because it was not the old man
who troubled me,
but his Evil Eye.

And every morning when the day broke,
I went boldly into his room,
and spoke bravely to him.
I called him cheerfully by his name,
and asked him
how he had passed the night.

So you see,
he would have been
a very clever old man indeed
to suspect that every night,
just at twelve,
I looked in on him while he slept.

Upon the eighth night
I was more than usually careful
in opening the door.
The minute hand on a clock
moves more quickly than mine did.
Never before that night
had I felt so powerful,
or so clever.

I could hardly contain myself.

To think that there I was,
opening the door,
little by little,
and he did not even dream
of my secret thoughts or deeds.

I fairly chuckled at the idea,
and I think he heard me,
because he suddenly moved on the bed
as if he was startled.

Now you may think that I drew back
– but no!

His room was as black as pitch
in thick darkness, so I knew
he could not see the door opening.
So I kept on,
pushing it open steadily, steadily.

I had my head in,
and was about to open the lantern,
when my thumb slipped.
The old man sprang up in bed,
and cried out, 'Who's there?'

I kept quite still,
and said nothing.

For a whole hour
I did not move a muscle.

I did not hear him lie down.
He was still
sitting up in bed listening –
just as I have done,
night after night,
listening to death
watching me from the walls.

This sounds
very strange,
but remember Poe
knew all about
strange dreams and
nightmares.

stifled –
choked back

And then I heard a slight groan,
and I knew it was
the groan of mortal terror.
It was not a groan of pain
or grief – oh no! –
it was the low stifled groan
that comes from the bottom of the soul
when it's filled with terror.

I knew the sound well.

Many nights, just at midnight,
when all the world slept,
I have felt it in my own soul.

I say I knew it well.
I knew what the old man felt.
And I pitied him,
although I chuckled at heart.

I knew that he had been lying awake
ever since the first slight noise,
when he had turned in his bed.
His fears had been
growing on him ever since.
He had been trying to say
there was nothing there,
but he couldn't.

He had been trying to say,
'It is nothing
but the wind in the chimney.'
– or 'It is only a mouse
crossing the floor.'
He had been trying to comfort himself,
but it was all in vain.

All in vain!

Because Death was nearing him,
was stalking him with its dark shadow.
And it was this shadow
that caused him to feel,
to *feel* the presence of my head
in the room.

I had waited a long time,
very patiently,
without hearing him lie down.

I decided to open the lantern
a very, very little.
So I opened it –
you cannot imagine
how stealthily, stealthily –
until a single dim ray,
like the thread of a spider,
shot out full upon the vulture eye.

stealthily – very quietly

It was open – wide, wide open,
and it made me angry as I gazed upon it.
I saw it perfectly clearly –
all a dull blue,
with a hideous veil over it
that chilled the marrow in my bones.

hideous – horribly ugly

But I could see nothing else
of the old man's face –
I had directed the ray as if by instinct,
right upon the damned spot.

As I've said before,
what you call madness
is no more than extra sharp senses.
Because now there came to my ears
a low dull quick sound,
like the ticking of a watch
wrapped in cotton wool.

I knew *that* sound well too.
It was the beating
of the old man's heart.

It made me even more angry,
just as the beating of a drum
makes a soldier brave.

But still I held back and kept quiet.
I scarcely breathed.
I held the lantern still,
and kept the light steadily
upon the eye.

Meanwhile the hellish
beat of his heart increased.
It grew quicker and quicker,
and louder and louder every instant.
The old man's terror
must have been extreme.
It grew louder, louder every moment.
And now at the dead hour of the night,
in the dreadful silence of
that old house, it terrified me.

Yet still, for some minutes longer,
I held back and stood still.

But the beating grew louder, louder!
I thought the heart must burst.

And now a new fear came to me –
the sound would be heard
by a neighbour!

The old man's hour had come!

With a loud yell,
I threw open the lantern
and leapt into the room.

He shrieked once – only once!

... to suffocate the old man

In an instant
I dragged him to the floor,
and pulled the heavy bed over him.
I then smiled cheerfully,
now that I had got so far.

But, for many minutes,
the heart beat on with a muffled sound.
But this didn't worry me –
it would not be heard through the wall.

At length it stopped.

The old man was dead.
I removed the bed
and examined the body.

Yes, he was stone, stone dead.
I placed my hand on the heart
and held it there many minutes.
There was no beat.
He was stone dead.
His eye would trouble me no more.

If you still think I'm mad,
then you will no longer
when I tell you how clever I was
in hiding the body.

The night was drawing on,
and I worked quickly, but in silence.

dismembered – cut into pieces

First of all I dismembered the body.
I cut off the head and the arms
and the legs.

I then took up three planks
from the floor,
and put everything in the space beneath.
I then put the boards back
so cleverly, so cunningly,
that no human eye – not even his –
could have seen anything wrong.

There was nothing to wash out –
no stain of any kind –
no blood at all.
I had been too careful for that.
A tub had caught it all – ha! ha!

When I had finished my work,
it was four o'clock –
still dark as midnight.

As the clock chimed the hour,
there came a knocking
at the street door.

I went down to open it
with a light heart –
what had I to fear now?

It was three men.

They were very polite.
They were police officers.
A neighbour had heard a shriek.
Foul play was suspected,
and they had been sent
to search the house.

I smiled – for what had I to fear?
I welcomed them in.
The shriek, I said,
was me having a nightmare.
The old man, I said,
was away in the country.

I took them all over the house.
I told them to search – search *well*.

I led them, at length,
to his room.

I showed them his gold
secure, undisturbed.
I even brought chairs in,
and asked them to sit and rest,
while I, in my wild confidence,
put my own chair upon the very spot
under which lay the body of the victim.

wild confidence – he feels very sure of himself

The officers were satisfied.
My manner had convinced them.
I was very at ease.
They sat,
and while I answered cheerily,
they chatted of familiar things.

familiar – ordinary

But, before long,
I felt myself getting pale
and wished them gone.
My head ached,
and a ringing started in my ears.
But still they sat and still chatted.

The ringing became clearer.
It carried on
and became clearer and clearer.

I talked more freely
to get rid of the feeling,
but it carried on
and grew stronger and stronger.

And then I found the ringing
was *not* in my ears.

urgently – insistently

I now grew very pale.
But I talked more urgently,
and more loudly.
Yet the sound grew worse.
What could I do?
It was *a low dull quick sound,*
like the ticking of a watch
wrapped in cotton wool!

I gasped for breath –
and yet the men heard it not.

I talked more quickly, and loudly,
but the noise grew worse.

I got up and argued about nothing,
in an excited voice,
waving my arms around,
but the noise grew worse.

Why *would* they not be gone?

I paced the floor to and fro
with heavy strides,
as if the men watching me
made me mad,
but the noise grew worse.

Oh God! What *could* I do?

I foamed –
I raved –
I swore!
I swung the chair
on which I had been sitting,
and smashed it on the boards,
but the noise grew worse and worse
above everything else.

It grew louder – louder – *louder!*

And still the men chatted pleasantly,
and smiled.
Was it possible they could not hear it?

Almighty God! – no, no!

They heard –
they suspected –
they *knew!*

They were laughing at me!
They were mocking me!

Anything would be better than this.
Anything would be easier
than them laughing at me.
I could bear those two-faced smiles
no more.
I felt that I must scream or die!

– and now – again! – listen!
louder! louder! louder! *louder!* –

'Villains!' I shrieked.
'Pretend no more!
I admit the deed! –
tear up the planks! –
here, here! –
it is the beating of his hideous heart!'

The Half Brothers
The Withered Arm
The Yellow Wallpaper
The Signalman
Boots at the Holly Tree Inn
The Well at Pen-Morfa
A Warning to the Curious
The Celebrated Jumping Frog of Calaveras County
On the Western Circuit